1964
Isle of Man
Railways & Recollections

Contents

Introduction	3
The Douglas Horse Tramway	4
The Manx Electric Railway	6
The Snaefell Mountain Railway	12
Personal Recollections	14, 16, 29, 36, 39, 45
The Isle of Man Steam Railway	
Busy times at Douglas	14
Locos on shed at Douglas	24
All aboard for Port Erin	27
Arrival at Port Erin	31
Catch it while you can	
Douglas to Ramsey	35
St John's	37
Ramsey	41
Peel to Douglas	43
Groudel Glen	47

Series Introduction

Welcome to a brand new and innovative series!

Railway publishing has been around almost as long as the railways themselves and there have been countless books with a historical theme, telling the story of a particular line, say, and occasionally linking the subject to its social context, but never before has there been, in such an accessible way, a juxtapositioning of photographic illustration of a railway subject with the events, happenings and highlights of a wider sphere and calendar. This series will, initially, take a particular year and place the views displayed alongside a carefully selected pot-pourri of what happened in that twelve-month period. The vast majority of the images in the first few books are from the Ray Ruffell collection, held by the publisher, but material from other sources will be interspersed where felt necessary to maintain appropriate variety. Ray was a railwayman and photographer of equal merit and the main criterion for inclusion in these books is for the images to be both interesting and aesthetically pleasing within a chosen theme.

The books are aimed at a more general market than mere railway aficionados or enthusiasts and the authors hope and trust that they will be sure in their aim and that you, the reader, will find much to enjoy, appreciate, enthuse about and even smile about! And it is hoped that some of your own memories are stirred along the way and that you may wish to share these with friends!

© John Stretton and Peter Townsend 2006
Photos: © The NOSTALGIA Collection archive unless otherwise credited.

All rights reserved. No part of this publication may be reproduced, stored in a retrieval system or transmitted, in any form or by any means, electronic, mechanical, photocopying, recording or otherwise, without prior permission in writing from Silver Link Publishing Ltd.

First published in 2006
ISBN 1 85794 278 7   ISBN 978 1 85794 278 1
Silver Link Publishing Ltd
The Trundle
Ringstead Road
Great Addington
Kettering
Northants NN14 4BW

Tel/Fax: 01536 330588
email: sales@nostalgiacollection.com
Website: www.nostalgiacollection.com
British Library Cataloguing in Publication Data
A catalogue record for this book is available from the British Library.

Printed and bound in Great Britain

Frontispiece **DOUGLAS:** The Island runabout ticket in 1964 cost just 15 shillings for a whole week, a point that no one visiting the Railway Station at Douglas could surely miss! This view taken from Atholl Street at 5.55 pm on 23rd August 1964, shows the imposing entrance to the impressive station building.

Above The Isle of Man Railway Company Crest from the side of No 10 Maitland.

Opposite background **PEEL:** Loco No 8 Fenella and crew awaiting departure on a train to Douglas on 25 August 1964

Introduction
Isle of Man Railways & Recollections 1964

As with any year, 1964 was a mixture of good and bad, important and trivial (in some eyes!), world events, political and social change and, on the UK's railways, a continuation of great upheaval following the twin prongs of the 1955 Modernisation Plan – and the introduction of dieselisation – and the Beeching Plan – to close many hundreds of miles of our railway system. A fate that was also to befall selected Isle of Man lines before the end of the 1960s.

A potentially explosive incident took place between the USA and North Korea in the Gulf of Tonkin; China exploded her first atomic bomb; Nelson Mandela was imprisoned in South Africa for opposing Apartheid; and, in America, the Surgeon General warned against the dangers of cigarette smoking! In the UK, The Beatles were still 'on the up', with their memorable trips to the USA, Australia and New Zealand; and, on the roads, the first Ford Mustang was produced. January 3rd saw the 72nd birthday of J R R Tolkien, whose books The Hobbit and Lord of the Rings were just beginning to gather cult reading status amongst University students, having been largely ignored since their publication many years earlier. July 21st was the 18th birthday of Cat Stevens, later to become a hit singer/songwriter before converting to Islam; and August 3rd was the 21st birthday of one of your authors!

Musically, the year started with The Dave Clark Five feeling Glad All Over at No.2 in the Charts and ended with The Beatles' appropriately titled I Feel Fine racing to become the sixth in their incredible run of eleven consecutive No.1 hits! In between, there were No.1's for The Bachelors (Diane), The Four Pennies (Juliet), The Animals (The House of the Rising Sun), The Rolling Stones (It's All Over Now), and Roy Orbison (Oh, Pretty Woman). Radio Caroline launched their broadcasting challenge to the BBC at Easter, out on the ocean waves, with The Rolling Stones' Not Fade Away; the Olympic Games took place in Tokyo; Mods and Rockers 'enjoyed' their skirmishes at various seaside resorts; My Fair Lady and Mary Poppins took the lion's share of the Oscars; and at Wembley on 14th May, West Ham United beat Preston North End 3-2 in the F A Cup.

On the railways, line closures that had slightly accelerated during 1963, literally went into overdrive this following year, with no fewer than 362 services, lines or parts of lines ended – virtually one per day for the whole year! Among these were the closure of the ex-M&SWJR route between Swindon Town and Cirencester Watermoor on (appropriately) April Fool's Day (!); withdrawal of passenger services over the two branches from Kemble five days later; passengers between Northampton (Castle) and Peterborough (East); closure of ex-LNW Seaton to Uppingham and ex-GNR Humberstone-Melton Mowbray North routes; passengers from Barry (Town) to Bridgend; closure between Caernarfon-Llanberis; and the ex-DN&SR 'cross-country' route from Didcot to Newbury. Readers will no doubt have their own 'favourites'!

This volume is illustrated with a series of pictures taken during August 1964 by *Ray Ruffell*. To the authors' knowledge none of these images have been published before.

Your authors hope you enjoy the mix and will, like Oliver, come back for more!

Peter Townsend
Northamptonshire

John Stretton
Oxfordshire

April 2006

DOUGLAS: The horse tram makes steady progress along the promenade. The gentleman on the pavement is keeping an eye on progress, or perhaps exchanging a few words with the tram driver. Car 18 seats 20 inside and 8 outside according to the sign to the left of the driver.

1964
The Douglas Horse Tramway

Opened on 7 August 1876 the Douglas Horse Tramway was the brainchild of Thomas Lighfoot, a retired civil engineer from Sheffield. Running from Burnt Mill Hill (later Summerhill) and a Pier (built 1869) that once stood at the bottom of Broadway, the line was extended to Peveril Square a stones throw from the potentially lucrative steamer piers.

Passing first in 1882 to a syndicate which evolved as Isle of Man Tramways Ltd., ownership was to pass through the hands of the Douglas & Laxey Coast Electric Tramway Co Ltd., and its succesor The Isle of Man Tramways & Electric Power Co Ltd., before eventually being purchased from the liquidators of the aforementioned, by Douglas Corporation Tramways.

Left **DOUGLAS:** Under the watchful eye of what appears to be an inspector striding across the forecourt, Car No 4 is seen entering the Derby Castle Horse Tram Depot on 23 August. The caption on the original photograph reads 'Changing Engines' - 'Hay Burner'! The Strathallan Hotel has 'Bass on draft' - this hotel was originlly Strathallan Lodge, built by Captain Pollock along with Derby Castle.

1964
Manx Electric Railway from Ramsey

Below **RAMSEY:** Of course it is still possible to visit Ramsey from Douglas by rail, by way of the MER. On 25 August we find the 11.30 from Ramsey to Douglas crossing Queens Drive in Ramsey having shortly before left from the then new station, seen here *(right)* with Motor Car No 19 in the far background.

Manx Electric Railway from Ramsey

Below **RAMSEY:** Motor Car No 19, toastrack car and box van wait patiently for passengers on 23 August at Ramsey terminus. This will be the 10.30am departure for Douglas.

Above **BALDRINE** Aboard the 8.20am from Ramsey to Douglas, we see the 8.50 departure from Douglas to Ramsey about to pass us.

DHON GLEN: A study in concentration as the driver of the 1.45pm Manx Electric Railway (MER) train from Ramsey to Douglas passes the 602 foot summit between Dhon Glen and Laxey on 23rd August.

Right **DOUGLAS:** Motor Car No 26 (built 1898) and Trailer Car No 56 (built 1904) are clearly expecting inclement weather as the shutters are firmly closed. Both cars are carrying their age well - a tribute to the hard work and dedication that has kept these cars running for upwards of 60 years.

Trailer car No 56 was to be rebuilt during 1994/95 as a saloon fully glazed with sides and was fitted out for disabled access, including removable seats, to provide for greater access and flexibility in service.

Left **LAXEY BAY:** The view from the 1.45 pm service from Ramsey to Douglas looking out over the bay. The traction poles are each numbered, which of course makes sense from a maintenance point of view, but these numbers are also used by staff as geographical markers. The 'old hands' take pride in knowing these numbers and their location to advise passengers of points of interest along the way. Is this the Manx equivalent of the London Cabbie's 'The Knowledge' one wonders?

1964
Members of The House of Keys during the year

Corkhill Thomas Ffinlo	1946 - 1966	
Kerruish Henry Charles	1946 - 1990	
Kelly Ambrose Spencer	1946 - 1966	
Coole Thomas Arthur	1950 - 1965	
Quayle William Ewan	1956 - 1970	
Crowe Edwin Norman	1956 - 1970	
Simcocks Alfred Howard	1956 - 1974	
Callister John Edward	1956 - 1971	
Stephen Robert Cannell	1956 - 1964	
Cain James Mylchreest	1956 - 1966	
Kaneen William Bowman	1956 - 1966	
Cain Harold Stanley	1958 - 1966	
Corkish Thomas Albert	1958 - 1971	
Gale George Crossley	1958 - 1964	
Colebourn Thomas Harold	1960 - 1966	
Coupe Percy	1962 - 1966	
Creer John Robert	1962 - 1981	
Kerruish Robert Edward Swain	1962 - 1970	
Kneale George Victor Harris	1962 - 1974	
MacLeod Hugh Duncan Campbell	1962 - 1976	
Matthews Cyril Harcourt	1962 - 1966	
Moore Eric Roy	1962 - 1966	
Sugden Sir Henry Haskins Clapham	1962 - 1976	
Radcliffe Percy	1963 - 1980	
Bell John James	1964 - 1966	
Quirk John Henry	1964 - 1965	

DOUGLAS: On 23 August, Motor Car No 22 is seen at Derby Castle Terminus with trailer car, believed to be No 37. The 48 seat Car No 22 was built in 1899 by George F Milnes of Birkenhead. Car No 22 was sadly all but destroyed by fire on the night of 30 September 1990. Thankfully she returned to service in 1992 with new bodywork by McArds of Port Erin.

The Manx Electric Railway

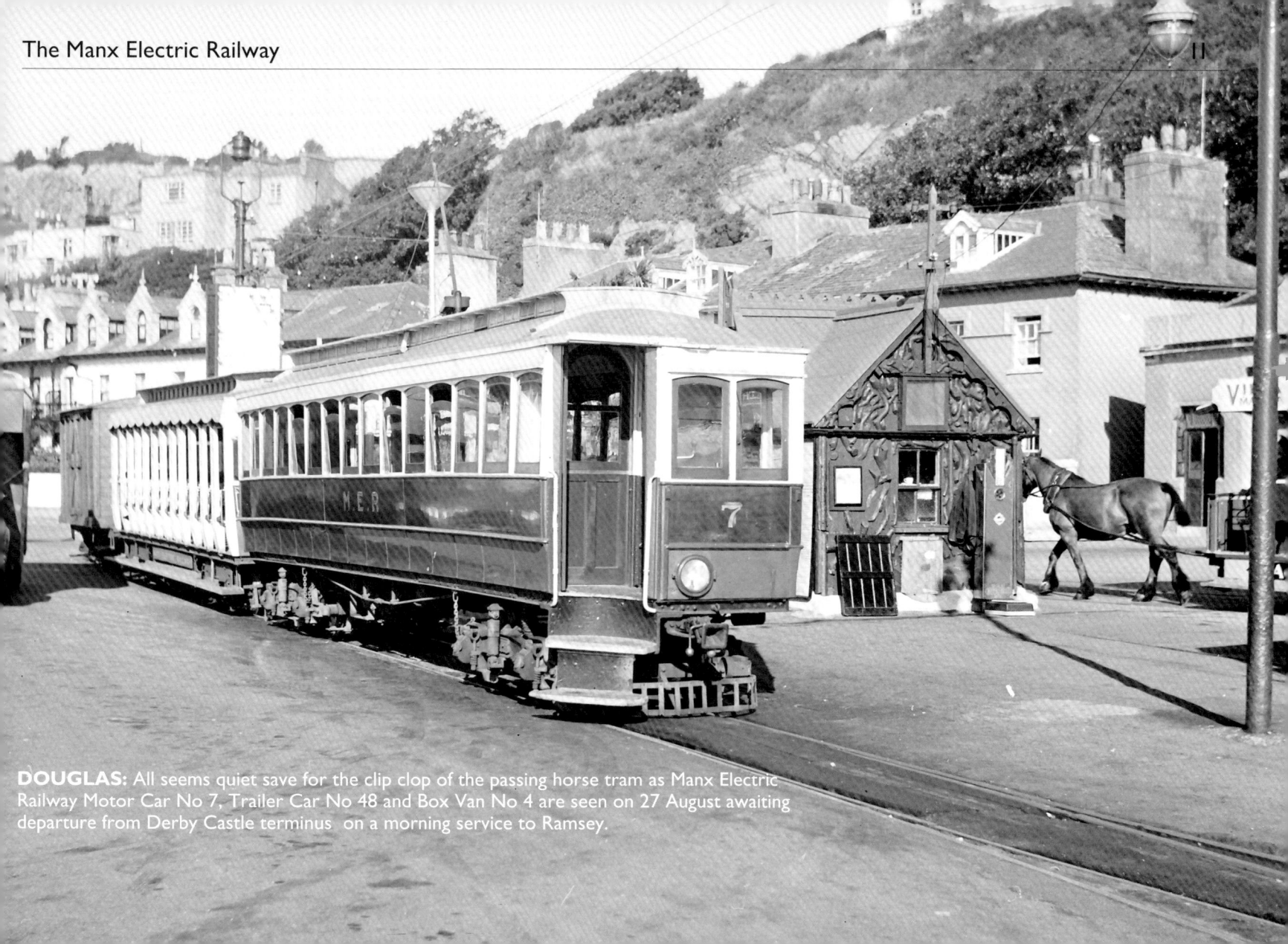

DOUGLAS: All seems quiet save for the clip clop of the passing horse tram as Manx Electric Railway Motor Car No 7, Trailer Car No 48 and Box Van No 4 are seen on 27 August awaiting departure from Derby Castle terminus on a morning service to Ramsey.

Above **LAXEY** This is where the Snaefell Mountain railway starts its climb to the summit of Snaefell some 2.036 feet above sea level. *Manx Electric Railway* Motor Car No 2 is seen passing *Snaefell Mountain Railway* Motor Car No 6.

Right **SNAEFELL SUMMIT:** The weather is closing in again as car No 4 arrives at the summit. Not surprisingly there is plenty of room on the bench, in spite of the fact that this is late summer - 28 August.

1964
The Snaefell Mountain Railway

**THIS CAR GOES TO THE SUMMIT OF SNAEFELL
FINE VIEW OF BIG WHEEL
HOTEL & REFRESMENT ROOMS ON SUMMIT OF MOUNTAIN**

So reads the advertising board on the roof of Motor Car No 6, which is seen here nearing the summit on 28 August. Rain clouds are gathering, and one wonders if the views on this particular day will be all that fine!

1964
Isle Of Man TT
1st, 2nd and 3rd

Lightweight 125cc
1st	Luigi Taveri	Honda
2nd	Jim Redman	Honda
3rd	Ralph Bryans	Honda

Sidecar TT
1st	Max Deubel	BMW
2nd	Colin Seeley	FCSB
3rd	Georg Auerbacher	BMW

Lightweight 250 TT
1st	Jim Redman	Honda
2nd	Alan Shepherd	MZ
3rd	Alberto Pagani	Paton

Junior TT
1st	Jim Redman	Honda
2nd	Phil Read	AJS
3rd	Mike Duff	AJS

50cc TT
1st	Hugh Anderson	Suzuki
2nd	Ralph Bryans	Honda
3rd	I Morishita	Suzuki

Senior TT
1st	Mike Hailwood	MV Agusta
2nd	Derek Minter	Norton
3rd	Fred J Stevens	Matchless

1964
The Isle of Man Steam Railway
Busy times at Douglas

Previous page **DOUGLAS:** *On your marks, get set...!* No 12 Hutchinson, No 8 Fenella and No 5 Mona line up at Douglas on 28 August 1964

Opposite **DOUGLAS:** The first line to be built out of Douglas was the eleven and a half mile route to Peel via St John's built in 1872/3. The railway was built by The Isle of Man Railway Company to a gauge of 3'0" due to the tight curves and often mountainous nature of the island.

This section was opened on 3 July 1873 and the Loco seen here No 5 Mona was delivered the following year 1874. The fact that she is still running in service on 28 August 1964 is a credit to her builders *Beyer Peacock & Co.*. She is at the time of writing (April 2006) still residing on the Island in the hands of the *Isle of Man Railway & Tramway Preservation Society*. One hopes that one day soon she will return to active service.

This view was taken from the signalbox and is looking across the tracks to the works building on the roof of which can be seen the large water tanks and the home signal gantry controlling the entrance to all platform roads.

On the right No 16 Mannin is on station pilot duties the crew can be seen keeping a watchful eye 'fore and aft' as she backs down towards the platforms.

1964
Arrivals & Departures

Births

Nicolas Cage	*actor*	7 January
Bridget Fonda	*actress*	27 January
Christopher Eccleston	*actor*	16 February
Matt Dillon	*actor*	18 February
Juliette Binoche	*actress*	9 March
Prince Edward		10 March
Shane Richie	*actor*	10 March
Martin Donnelly	*racing driver*	26 March
Russell Crowe	*actor*	7 April
Adrian Moorhouse	*swimmer*	24 May
Kathy Burke	*actress/comedienne*	13 June
Johnny Herbert	*racingdriver*	25 June
Bonnie Langford	*actress*	22 July
Sandra Bullock	*actress*	26 July
Jim Corr	*singer/musician*	31 July
Keanu Reeves	*actor*	2 September

Deaths

Alan Ladd,	*actor*	(b. 1913)	29 January
Peter Lorre	*actor*	(b. 1904)	23 March
Jawaharlal Nehru	*PM of India*	(b. 1889)	27 May
Jim Reeves	*singer*	(b. 1923)	31 July
Sean O'Casey	*writer*	(b. 1880)	18 September
Harpo Marx	*comedian*	(b. 1888)	28 September
Cole Porter	*composer*	(b. 1891)	15 October
Herbert Hoover	*31st US President*	(b. 1874)	29 October
Sam Cooke	*singer*	(b. 1931)	11 December
Robert Cannell Stephen	*Member House Keys*	(b. 1902)	31 January

(Member of the Executive Council, elected in 1956 to represent South Douglas and was the first chairman of the Finance Board)

Busy times at Douglas

DOUGLAS: No 16 Mannin is being kept busy! Here we see her shunting freight vans on 28 August, again under the watchful eye of the crew member who is perhaps thanking his partner on the footplate for the steam cleaning of his boots!

How many people remember *Jewsbury & Brown's Mineral Waters* seen being advertised on the enamel sign fixed to the works building wall? *Jewsbury & Brown* were a Manchester firm which was started in the 1820's and was taken over by *Schweppes* in 1964 - the same year in which this photograph was taken.

Busy times at Douglas

DOUGLAS: A fine view of the station approach at Douglas. No 16 Mannin is still busily shunting away in the background. All visible signals are set to danger indicating that no arrivals or departures are due. The bracketed signal gantry the base of which we saw in the earlier shot can now be seen in its entirety. The signal box commands an excellent view from its position next to the carriage and wagon sheds seen on the right. Someone seems to have left a barrel in a rather dangerous position on the right hand carriage shed road!

Busy times at Douglas

Left **DOUGLAS:** The signalman's view shortly after 10 am on 28 August as No 12 Hutchinson is seen backing down to her train waiting in Platform 2. No 12 was built by *Beyer Peacock & Co.* in 1908 and remains in service at the time of writing (April 2006), so this grand old timer is just two years away from her 100th birthday - perhaps a telegram from the Queen?

A train has just arrived in Platform 4, far left, and the train engine is seen emerging from behind the carriages having just run round ready to go on shed for servicing before the next tour of duty.

No 16 Mannin is shunting carriage stock on Platform 3 in which three carriages are already waiting.

Below **DOUGLAS:** A peep behind the carriage sheds at Douglas on 28 August reveals derelict rolling stock stored out of use including Brake Van E5 a very early four wheeler.

Busy times at Douglas

Far left **DOUGLAS:** A quiter moment at Douglas on 27 August. Station Pilot No 16 Mannin has just delivered empty coaching stock to platform 2 and is moving off towards the carriage sheds. What appears to be an eager train-spotter can be seen just to the right of the Platform 1 home starter signal. On close examination he appears to be writing in a pocket book - or perhaps not!

left **DOUGLAS:** On 27 August we see No 10 G.H. Wood arriving at Douglas on the 10.35 am departure from Port Erin.

The line from Port Erin and Castletown was added to the system in 1874 opening in August of that year.

The car on the extreme right appears to be a Hillman Minx (Phase 5) first introduced in 1951 and from the appearnce is clearly very well cared for! Behind the Minx can be seen the front end of one of the Ex-*County Donegal Railway* diesel railcars, of which more later.

On the left can be seen the Douglas signal box from which trails interlocking point rodding and signal wires. The signal box reminds your author very much of the Midland Railway boxes now rapidly disappearing from his home patch of the East Midlands.

1964
Locos on shed at Douglas

left **DOUGLAS:** One of the original three Locos No 1 Sutherland built in 1873 by *Beyer Peacock & Co.* is seen here outside Douglas loco shed on 27 August 1964. The other two original Locos were No 2 Derby (Scrapped) and No 3 Pender.

Loco No 3 Pender can still be seen today, but not on the Isle of Man. The Manchester Museum of Science and Industry recognising the fact that this Loco was a product of the city based *Beyer, Peacock and Co.* purchased the Loco and it is now on display in cut away form at the museum. Sadly old No 1 is no longer in service although at the time of writing it is still extant all be it partially dismantled.

Right **DOUGLAS:** Loco No 5 Mona is seen here on 24 August at the end of a hard working day. Note piles of ash - a feature of loco disposal - the fireman can be seen on the footplate and leaning against the cab are two tools of his trade, the irons used to clear the ash from the firebox. Note also the now very old fashioned looking mechanical digger - a time saving means of loading coal and clearing all the resulting ash!

1964
All aboard for Port Erin

Left **DOUGLAS:** Platform 2 on the 24 August sees No 11 Maitland waiting patiently for passengers to Port Erin. On Platform 3 we see Ex-*County Donegal Railway* diesel railcars Nos 19 & 20 awaiting departure with the 2.05 pm departure for Peel. These railcars were purchased by the railway in 1961 and were built in 1950/51 by *Walker Brothers* of Wigan. They are currently in store following withdrawal under a scheme to renovate and restore them during the 1990's.

Sadly the work proved too extensive and costly and was abandoned when partially completed. Much favoured by enthusiasts and modellers - for whom they represent a challenge - one hopes that one day they may once again be seen in service.

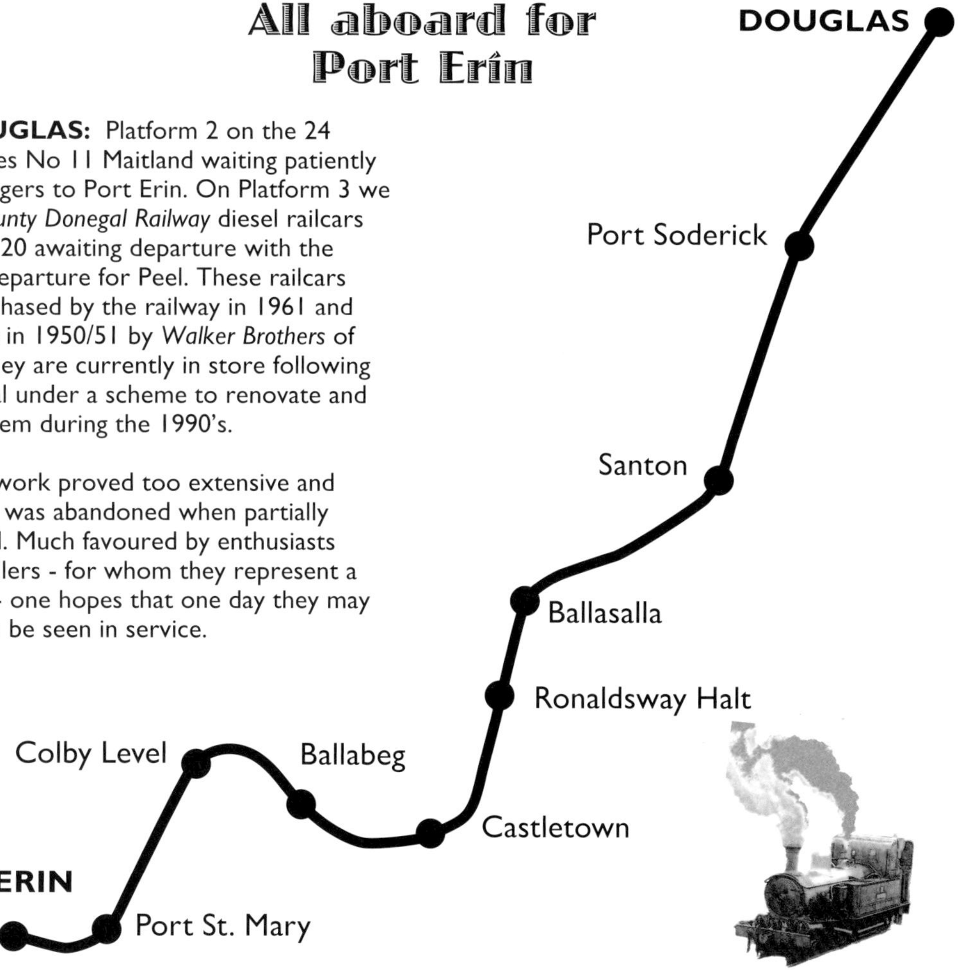

Left **DOUGLAS:** The 10.30 am departure for Port Erin has a good head of steam as she takes the left hand track out of Douglas. Sadly it is no longer possible to travel on the right hand route out of Douglas to Peel, St Johns and connecting services to Ramsey and in very early years to Foxdale.

Right **DOUGLAS:** Swinging the camera round to follow the train we see the line to Port Erin begin to climb above the erstwhile line to Peel.

In the distance can be seen the chimney and, just visible in the steam, a cooling tower of the power station at Pulrose. Dating back to 1928 the power station suffered badly from flooding during 1930, when the power station even closed down for a period as a result. The station was enlarged in 1935 work having been carried out to ease the likelyhood of further problems with flooding. In the early years of electric power on the island, the MER not only generated power for its own needs but was one of many private companies that supplied power to other homes and businesses.

Since this picture was taken this Power station has been swept away and replaced with a hi-tech power generating plant that features a magnificent 30m glazed generating hall and at night has a remarkable lighting feature. Water remains a feature but is now incorporated in the aesthetically pleasing design!

1964
Happenings (1)

Wimbledon
   Roy Emerson beats Fred Stolle
   to win Men's Singles Final:
   6-4, 12-10, 4-6, 6-3   July
   Maria Bueno beats Margaret Smith
   to win Women's Singles Final:
   6-4, 7-9 6-3   July

Donald Campbell (1)
   sets record for turbine vehicle,
   690.91 kph (429.31 mph)   July

Fred Trueman
   takes 300th Test wicket (Neil Hawke)
   England vs Australia at The Oval   August

Vatican
   abolished Latin as official language
   of Roman Catholic liturgy   November

Donald Campbell (2)
   sets world water speed record
   276.33 mph   December

The FA Cup 1963/4 (over two legs)
   West Ham win   West Ham 3 - 2 Stoke

The League Cup 1963/4 (over two legs)
   Leicester City win   Leicester 1 - 1 Stoke
                             Leicester 3 - 2 Stoke

Left **PORT SODERICK:** Is that one Guard or two? The Guard of the 2.15 pm departure from Douglas on 24 August, hauled by No 11 Maitland, is reflecting perhaps in more ways than one, not only is he reflected in the carriage window but also seems to be reflecting on some aspect of yet another photographer capturing what to him was all in a days work. To many railway enthusiast an opportunity to visit the Isle of Man and capture scenes such as this were all too rare.

The Guard's friendly smile and smart appearance add considerably to this timeless snapshot in time. Interestingly the 2006 timetable still features a 2.15 pm departure to Port Erin and is scheduled to call at Port Soderick at 2.27 pm.

Right **PORT ERIN:** Having arrived at the terminus No 11 Maitland has uncoupled from her train and has moved forward and waits patiently for the fireman to change the points, by hand, before moving back past the carriages for servicing before coupling back up ready for the return journey to Douglas.

At the time of writing No 16 Mannin is on static display in the *Railway Museum* at Port Erin - well worth a visit!

1964
Arrival at Port Erin

PORT ERIN: A very smart looking No 12 Hutchinson running into Platform 1 at Port Erin to couple up to the 3.45 pm service to Douglas on 24 August. In the left background is the Port Erin Legion Hall. The Port Erin Branch of *The Royal British Legion* is one of 12 on the Island and I am very pleased to report is still going strong. Port Erin Legion is fortunate in having their own premises, which has recently been refurbished with a new floor and facilities for the disabled. Port Erin also has the largest membership of any branch on the Island. The branch have built a very nice Garden of Remembrance at the front of the hall which is cared for by Members of the Branch Committee and looks out over the railway lines. The Island's railways saw considerable use in both World Wars and many service men and women would have left from the station, sadly some would never return. The Garden of Remembrance being close to the railway is a poignant reminder - do please stay a while if visiting Port Erin.

The Secretary of over 35 years Ken Furniss recalls that in 1964 *Wilfred Pickles*, the well known broadcaster of the period, presented a programme from the Legion Hall - your author suspects this was probably an 'episode' of *Have a go* which was broadcast live from locations all over the country, and ran from 1946 to 1967 on the *BBC Light Programme*.

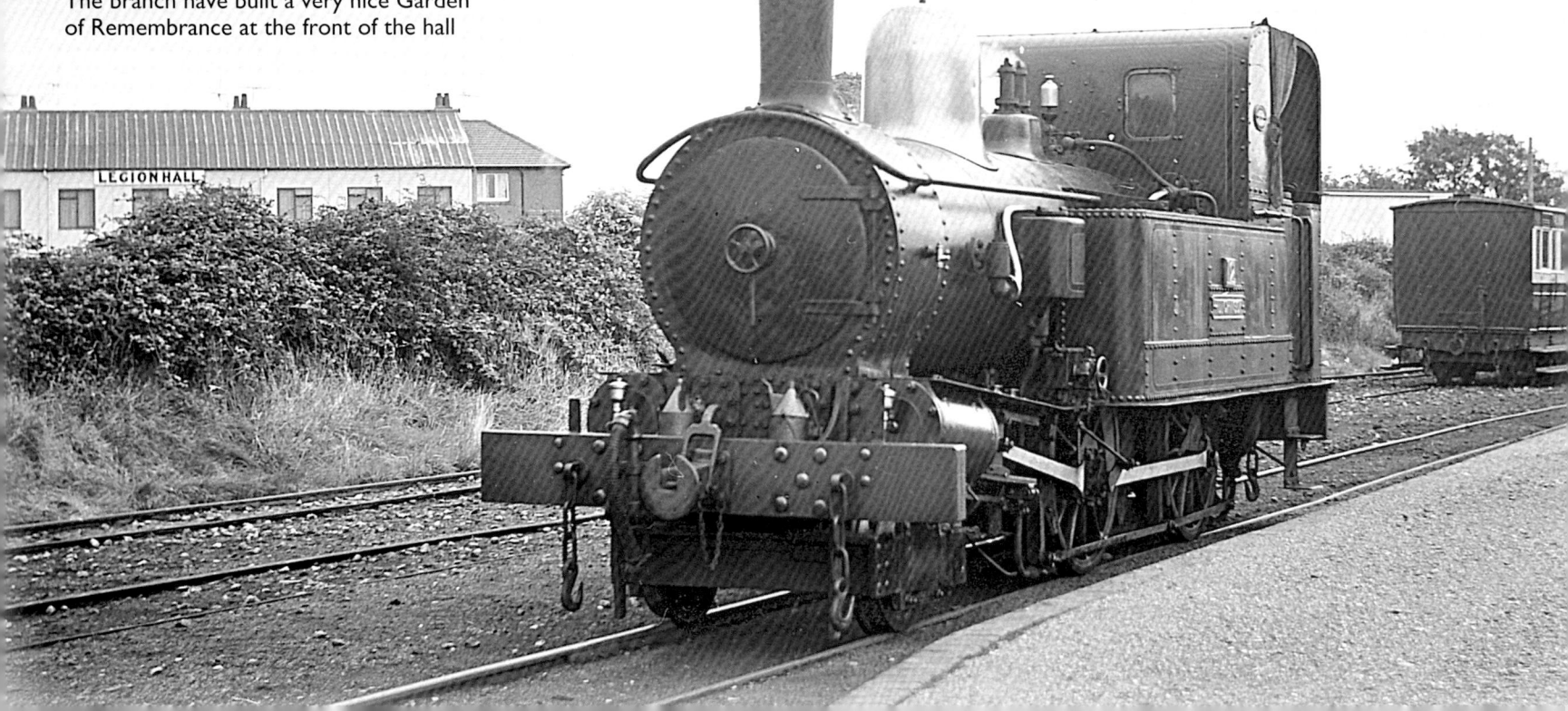

Arrival at Port Erin

Below **PORT ERIN:** This wonderful panoramic view of Port Erin, fashions and bus apart, could almost have been taken in Victorian times! In fact it is on 24 August 1964 and on the left we see the stock from the 2.15 pm from Douglas recently arrived behind No 11 Maitland. This will form the 4.10 pm departure to Douglas. On the right No 12 Hutchinson, having now coupled up, will be departing shortly with the 3.45 pm service to Douglas. Behind the bushes to the right of No 12 stands a Leyland Titan bus one of 18 purchased by Isle of Man Road services in 1949. When the first Double deckers arrived in the island around 1946 their use was restricted to Douglas and some ran with most of the top deck blocked off. This restriction was soon removed by the Manx Government and 'normal service' as one might say commenced!

The impressive building beyond the bus is *The Station Hotel* which is still very much in business, having been extensively refurbished during 2005/6.

Left **PORT ERIN:** Following arrival on a service from Douglas on 27 August Loco No 10 G. H. Wood is in need of minor attention at Port Erin loco shed. Closer examination of the photograph reveals that the loco is not the only item needing attention, the shed door is clearly in a poor state of repair! Note that the gentleman nearest the camera is holding that all important enamel pot so beloved of footplate crews. No self respecting footplateman would leave home without it, in the days of steam this would be kept in close proximity to the firebox, thereby keeping its contents as warm as possible!

Right **DOUGLAS:** Returning briefly to the outskirts of Douglas we pick up our train to Ramsey at the point seen previously on page 26. This time we are travelling on the right hand track out of Douglas behind No 8 Fenella on the 10. 25 am departure for Ramsey on 28 August 1964. This route was to close just 4 years later along with the line to Peel. The line to Foxdale was an earlier casualty having closed in 1940. The shortest lived section of line was the branch off the Peel to St John's route to *Knockaloe Camp.* This line was opened in 1915 to serve the internment camp for prisoners of war and those considered to be a risk to the nation during war time. The branch delivered tons of food and supplies to the camp during its short existence. The branch closed in 1920.

Catch it while you can - Douglas to Ramsey

1964 Catch it while you can! Douglas to Ramsey

Above **St. JOHN'S:** On 28 August No 5 Mona is in charge of the 12 noon departure from Douglas seen here having just arrived at St John's. She will be going forward shortly to Ramsey. Just visible to the right are the carriages of a Peel service. That box looks very heavy - the footplate crewman seems to be watching closely as the passenger struggles towards the open door. I reckon he would have been glad to put that down!

1964
Happenings (2)

Peter Sellers and Britt Ekland
  marry in London   19 February
Mods and Rockers
  clash at seaside resorts   Whitsun
Top of the Pops
  first broadcast   1st January
The Beatles first US album
  Meet the Beatles, is released   20 January
Jack Ruby found guilty
  of killing John F. Kennedy's assassin
  Lee Harvey Oswald   14 march
BBC2 Television
  starts broadcasting in the UK   20 April
Greville Wynn
  imprisoned in Moscow since 1963
  exchanged for Soviet spy
  Gordon Lonsdale.   22 April
Prime Minister Nehru of India
  dies; succeeded by Lal Shastri.   27 May
Nelson Mandela
  and seven others are sentenced
  to life imprisonment in South Africa
  and sent to prison   12 June
Last executions in the United Kingdom
  Gwynne Owen Evans and
  Peter Anthony Allen   13 August
Forth Road Bridge opens
  Firth of Forth in Scotland   4 September
Daily Herald ceases publication
  replaced by The Sun.   14 September

1964
Catch it while you can!
St John's

St. JOHN'S: Three days earlier on 25 August it seems to be all happening at St John's with trains on all visible roads bar one. On the left railcars Nos 19 & 20 are running in tandem, while next in the line up is 'old No 1' Sutherland. Completing the engines in view is No 8 Fenella

Catch it while you can - Douglas to Ramsey

Inset **St. JOHN'S:** On leaving St John's the lines to Peel on the left and to Ramsey on the right ran parallel for a short distance and on 28 August the 12 noon departures to both destinations are running neck and neck. This view taken from the train to Ramsey captures the driver of No 16 Mannin leaning out of the cab as he heads down the clear straight track towards Peel.

Main picture **St. JOHN'S:** Shortly after the inset view the tracks diverge and the line to Ramsey climbs gently away to the right. Here we see No 16 Mannin and it's train of two carriages and a sleeper wagon across the field scuttling along on route to Peel.

1964
Happenings (3)

Malta obtains independance
   from the United Kingdom   (21 September)
Summer Olympics
   open in Tokyo   (10 October)
Nikita Khrushchev
   ousted as Soviet Leader replaced by
   Leonid Brezhnev and Alexei Kosygin
                              (14/15 October)
Labour Party
   wins the election ending 13 years
   of Tory rule   (15 October)
Harold Wilson
   becomes Prime Minister   (16 October)
British Parliament
   votes to abolish the death penalty
   for murder in Britain   (9 November)
Cassius Clay (Muhammad Ali)
   takes world heavyweight boxing title
   from Sonny Liston.   (February)
First driverless trains
   run on London Underground   (April)
Ian Smith
   becomes premier of Rhodesia   (April)
Geoffrey Boycott
   makes his test debut England vs. Australia
   at Trent Bridge   (June)
The Beatles
   attend The Queen's birthday party   (June)

Above left **KIRK MICHAEL:** No 8 Fenella arrives at Kirk Michael on 25 August with the 1.45 pm Ramsey to Douglas. No 8 built by *Beyer, Peacock & Co* in 1894 is still in service today having been purchased by The Isle of Man Railway & Tramway Preservation Society

Right **RAMSEY:** No 5 Mona approaching Ramsey on the 12 noon departure from Douglas on 25 August.

1964
Catch it while you can!
RAMSEY

Right **RAMSEY:** Turning the camera round this is the view the driver of No 5 Mona would have seen as he neared journey's end at Ramsey. This route from St John;s to Ramsey was constructed by *J & W Grainger* of Glasgow and was built for the *Manx Northern Railway Company* (Formed - 1877) to the same 3' gauge employed by *The Isle of Man Railway Company*. There were extensive buildings here as can be seen with the carriage sheds on the left and the Loco shed beyond.

The line from St. Johns opened on 1 July 1879 with two 2-4-0T Locos purchased from Manchester based *Sharpe Stewart & Co.* They were designated No 1 Ramsey and No 2 Northern by the MNR, these were followed by two further Locos No 3 Thornhill* from *Beyer Peacock & Co.* in 1880 and 0-6-0T No 4 Caledonia*, built by *Dubs & Co.* in 1885. *The Manx Northern Railway* was absorbed by The IOMR in 1904 and all four Locos were taken over at this time. No 1 Ramsey was scrapped some 18 years later. No 2 Northern lasted only 8 further years until 1912.

Sadly the line to Ramsey closed completely just 4 short years after this photograph was taken. The last passenger train running on 6 September 1968.

* Renumbered 14 and 15 by IOMR

Above left **RAMSEY:** No 5 Mona arrives at Ramsey on the 12.00 noon departure from Douglas. One wonders if the passengers were listening to, or even aware that *Radio Caroline (North)* one of the many Pirate Radio stations that were springing up in the 1960's started broadcasting from a ship moored off Ramsey during 1964. Transistor radios were the 'lap tops', 'mobile phones' and 'MP3 players' of their day and your author well remembers the same adverse reactions from many to such things in railway compartments as we see to today's hi-tech devices! The then privately owned *Manx Radio* was granted a licence to broadcast to the Island in June 1964. Many thwarted attempts by entrepreneurs to gain a licence from the GPO in London had been made prior to this and even then *Manx Radio* was on a low frequency which neither reached all of the Island or competed for signal strength with the afore mentioned *Radio Caroline*.

Above right **RAMSEY:** No 8 Fenella has collected an extra carriage No F.14 for the 1.45 pm departure to Douglas on 25 August and is seen here propelling it towards the waiting stock. The long building seen in the background is the carriage shed seen in the earlier picture approaching Ramsey.

1964
Catch it while you can!
Peel to Douglas

PEEL: There are six carriages to choose from for the 4.25 pm departure from Peel on 25 August behind No 8 Fenella. This service had but a short time to live with the line closing in 1968. No doubt there will come a time when more than just railway enthusiasts will regret the passing of this transport corridor to Douglas much of which has of course now been built over.

Above PEEL: The Ex-*County Donegal Railway Company* railcars Nos 19 & 20 have just arrived at Peel. On the extreme left can be seen the ruins of Peel's St Germain's Cathedral which dates back to circa 1230 and was in use until the late 1700s, the last enthronement of a Bishop taking place in the cathedral in 1785. Final abandonment came in 1824 when as a result of a viscious storm the main roof was destroyed. The estury of the River Neb provides a safe haven for shipping and at one time business for the railway. The railcars will shortly be returning to Douglas and the land hereabouts will all too soon be developed and built on, a large car park now takes up much of the station area. There is however still a link with the railway in the form of an exhibition part of *The Manx Transport Museum*. which is to be found in the old Brickworks office in Mill Road.

Opposite **PEEL - St JOHN'S:** Leaving Peel behind this is the view from the carriage window as No 8 Fenella takes the 4.25 pm departure towards St John's and onwards to Douglas. Note how well groomed the track side bank and lineside appear in this picture; bearing in mind this is August much work must have been carried out to keep the foliage at bay!

1964
No 1 Records

January
I Want To Hold Your Hand — The Beatles
Glad All Over — The Dave Clark Five
Needles & Pins — The Searchers
February
Diane — The Bachelors
Anyone Who Had A Heart — Cilla Black
March
Little Children — Billy J. Kramer & The Dakotas
April
Can't Buy Me Love — The Beatles
A World Without Love — Peter & Gordon
May
Don't Throw Your Love Away — Searchers
Juliet — Four Pennies
You're My World — Cilla Black
June
It's Over — Roy Orbison
July
The House Of The Rising Sun — The Animals
It's All Over now — The Rolling Stones
A Hard Day's Night — The Beatles
August
Do Wah Diddy Diddy — Manfred Mann
Have I The Right — The Honeycombes
September
You Really Got Me — The Kinks
I'm Into Something Good — Herman's Hermits
October
Oh Pretty Woman — Roy Orbison
(There's) Always Something There To Remind Me — Sandie Shaw
November
Baby Love — The Supremes
December
Little Red Rooster — The Rolling Stones
I Feel Fine — The Beatles

DOUGLAS: Our final view of the steam railway shows No 10 G.H.Wood approaching Douglas with the 10.35 departure from Port Erin passing the works the signal indicating that she will arrive in Platform 3. Railway modellers will find much to inspire them in this shot, not least the signal gantry to the left and the roof detail on the right.

1964
Groudle Glen - Sea Lion awaits...

Right **GROUDEL GLEN:** The *Groudle Glen Railway* was constructed to cater for the increasing number of visitors wishing to visit the Zoo at Sea Lion Rocks. The Glen had seen a boom following the opening of the MER line to Laxey and a 2' gauge railway to transfer visitors from the top of the Glen at Lhen Coan down to the Zoo turned out to be an excellent decision. The railway opened on 23 May 1896 with a consist of just three carriages and one Loco a Bagnall built 2-4-0T *Sea Lion*. It was not long before a further engine *Polar Bear* also a 2-4-0T from Bagnalls was purchased along with more carriages.

Our picture taken on 24 August 1964 shows Sea Lion in the loco shed at Groudle Glen having suffered from an attack by vandals. The railway was closed at this time and *Sea Lion* was sold by the end of the decade. The tracks were scrapped in the early 1970s and it seemed that this wonderful railway had gone for ever.

However the *Isle of Man Steam Railway Supporters' Association* had different ideas and launched a restoration campaign in 1982 and remarkably by 1986 had re-opened a stretch of line from Lhen Coan to the headland. Perhaps even more remarkable is the fact that following a complete restoration over a two and a half year period by the apprentices at *BNFL* Training Centre at Sellafield in Cumbria, *Sea Lion* returned to the railway and entered service in October 1987. By 1993 the railway had been fully reinstated to Seal Lion Rocks.

Index

Acknowledgements	48
1964 The Isle of Man TT	14
1964 Arrivals & Departures	16
1964 Happenings (1)	29
1964 Happenings (2)	36
1964 Happenings (3)	39
1964 No 1 Records	45

LOCOMOTIVES AND ROLLING STOCK

DHT
Car No 4	5
Car No 18	4

GGR
Sea Lion	47

IOMSR
No 1 Sutherland	24
No 2 Derby	24
No 3 Pender	24
No 5 Mona	15, 17, 25, 36, 38, 40, 42
No 8 Fenella	15, 35, 37, 40, 42, 43, 45
No 10 G.H. Wood	23, 34, 46
No 11 Maitland	26, 30, 31
No 12 Hutchinson	15, 32, 33
No 16 Mannin	17, 18, 19, 20, 22
Railcar No 19	26, 37, 44
Railcar No 20	26, 37, 44

MER
Motor Car No 2	12
Motor Car No 7	11
Motor Car No 19	6, 7
Motor Car No 22	10
Motor Car No 26	9
Trailer Car No 48	11
Trailer Car No 56	9
Box Van No 4	11

MNR
No 1 Ramsey	41
No 2 Northern	41
No 3 Thornhill	41
No 4 Caledonia	41

SMR
Motor Car No 6	12, 13
Motor Car No 4	12

PLACES
Baldrine	7
Dhon Glen	8
Douglas	1, 4, 5, 9-11, 14, 15, 17-26, 28, 29, 35, 46
Groudel Glen	47
Kirk Michael	40
Knockaloe Camp	34
Laxey	12
Laxey Bay	8
Peel	43-45
Port Erin	31-34
Port Soderick	30
Ramsey	6, 7, 40-42
Snaefell Summit	12, 13
St. John's	36-39

Acknowledgements

First and foremost we would like to record our gratitude to the late Ray Ruffell without whom this book would not have been possible. Ray was a railwayman through and through and his interest went far beyond his day to day work, extending from minature railways through narrow gauge to the most obscure industrial railways. Ray travelled the length and breadth of the British Isles and many locations abroad in pursuit of his subject.

Thankfully for us, and indeed future generations, Ray was also an accomplished photographer. His extensive collection has been kept complete and forms an important part of the photographic archives of The NOSTALGIA Collection.
So many people have helped - with snippets and guidance, facts and information - space, and space alone, precludes mention of them all, so THANK YOU ALL!

By way of representing our gratitude to all here are just a few names...
Frances Townsend for sustaining her husband through the process. Audrey Brown, Honorary Secretary, Isle of Man County, The Royal British Legion for her enthusiastic and helpful responses to our various questions relating to Port Erin, to Jonathan Brooks for encouragement to add an Isle of Man title to the series, to Will Adams, Mick Sanders and David Walshaw for putting up with my (PT) constant wittering and a lot more besides!

Peter Rowlands a friend of PT for over 30 years and a credit to the world of publishing - *thanks mate!*